The Singer in the Stream

A STORY OF AMERICAN DIPPERS

Katherine Hocker and Mary Willson

Illustrations by Katherine Hocker

Yosemite Conservancy
YOSEMITE NATIONAL PARK

If you want to hear an American dipper singing, you'll need to be near a stream. That's because dippers—unique among all songbirds—spend their entire lives beside (and under!) the water. Their long, complicated songs can be heard even over the roaring of waterfalls. Dippers can sing both breathing out and breathing in . . . can you?

U p along the creek,
  where the water tumbles down,
There's a singer in the stream—
  a songster of renown—
Perching on the rocks
  with his long, strong toes,
Bobbing up and down
  where the clear water flows.

Dippers are named for the way they bob: up and down and up and down and up and down and . . .

. . . nobody (except a dipper) knows why they do this.

Caddisflies flutter over the water like moths, dipping down to lay their eggs.

A small gray bird
   with a big loud voice,
He dives in pools and waterfalls,
   and bugs are his choice.
Big bugs, little bugs,
   clinging to the stones—
They can't escape this hunter
   in the stream that he owns.

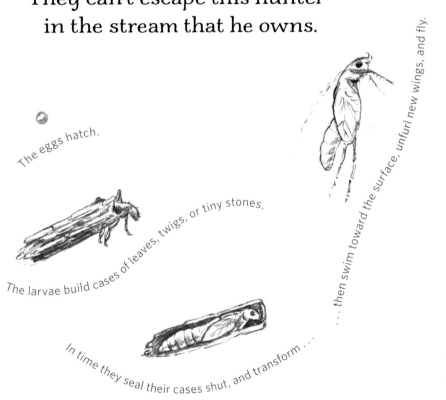

The eggs hatch.

The larvae build cases of leaves, twigs, or tiny stones.

In time they seal their cases shut, and transform . . .

. . . then swim toward the surface, unfurl new wings, and fly.

Dippers eat aquatic insects (insects that live underwater) such as caddisflies, mayflies, and stoneflies. They also eat small fish. Can you find at least four dipper foods in this picture? From left to right along the bottom are a salmon fry and two stoneflies. Above the stoneflies is a sculpin.

Other birds sometimes nest along
dipper streams: hermit thrushes,
Pacific wrens . . .

. . . belted kingfishers . . .

One day in early spring,
    very crisp and cool,
Another bird appears,
    swimming in his pool!
At first he isn't friendly,
    and chases her away.
Then they settle down,
    and she decides to stay.

. . . and harlequin ducks . . .

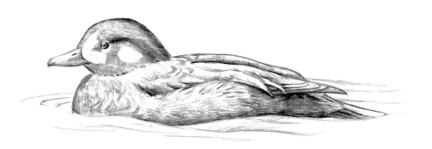

. . . but nobody builds a nest quite like a dipper's. There's
an old dipper nest in this picture. Can you find it? The old
nest looks like a clump of moss with a hollow in the top.
Look to the left of the waterfall, in the crack in the rock face.

If another dipper tries to feed or rest in their territory,
a dipper pair will fiercely drive it off.

The dippers own a bit of stream,
  sharing everything.
But they're feisty little fighters,
  especially in spring.
Let trespassers beware—
  these two will have their way.
Intruders get a beating
  and quickly fly away.

After the battle, they go back to diving for food,

sometimes pausing to s t r e t c h.

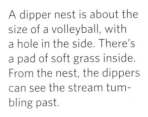

A dipper nest is about the size of a volleyball, with a hole in the side. There's a pad of soft grass inside. From the nest, the dippers can see the stream tumbling past.

They weave a mossy nest,
  weatherproof and warm,
Where Mama dipper lays her eggs,
  safe from flood and storm.
Four white eggs—
  she lays one every day,
Then settles in the ball of moss
  to keep the cold away.

Papa dipper brings her treats,
  a lovely bug or two,
Or for something special,
  a tiny fish will do.
Inside the toasty eggs,
  the little chicks are growing.
More than two weeks later,
  a wee head is showing.

When the eggs have hatched,
 the parents have to scurry.
Filling all those little mouths
 means hurry, hurry, hurry!
Little bugs first,
 then bigger ones later.
Chicks grow very fast,
 so parents have to cater.

Here's a tasty caddisfly,
 here's a little midge,
Here's a wiggling salmon fry,
 caught beneath the bridge.
The nest is getting crowded,
 beaks are gaping wide.
How could there be room
 for all those chicks inside?

· · · over and over, flying miles and miles, feeding hungry chicks from dawn to dusk.

For a while after the chicks hatch, the parents keep the nest tidy by carrying their droppings away. But eventually they stop doing that, so the nest entrance becomes streaked with droppings. As the chicks' pinfeathers grow in, their scaly coverings flake off and pile up inside the nest. The nest lining, which once was so soft, is now trampled and dirty. It's time to leave!

Three weeks later,
    the chicks are getting bold,
The nest is hot and stuffy,
    the stream looks clean and cold.
Out the door they bob their heads,
    peering at the ground.
They know they have to leave the nest—
    but it's a long way down!

As the time to leave the nest draws near, the parent birds stand in the stream below,

calling, calling, calling, calling, calling. . . .

The boldest pops out first
  and tumbles to the water.
She's followed by two others,
  with stubby wings aflutter.
Three fuzzy fledglings
  blinking in the light;
The fourth's still undecided
  (he'll make the leap tonight).

When the dipper fledglings make the leap from the nest, their wings are short and their tails are shorter. They've never flown before...but their fluttering wings help guide them and keep them from landing TOO hard. If they land in the water, they quickly paddle to a rock or log and scramble up.

M ama's job's not over,
and Papa's isn't either.
In fact, it's really tough for them—
no time to take a breather.
Two chicks fly upstream,
two go down the falls;
It takes a lot more effort now
to feed and watch them all!

For the first day or so after they leave the nest, dipper fledglings stay close by,
usually perched on rocks just below the nest. But soon they can fly well enough to
follow their parents up and down the stream. They beg almost constantly, fluttering
their wings and calling. This picture shows what a parent dipper sees all day long:
a big, gaping, yellow beak.

In addition to insects, dippers eat small fish such as sculpins and sticklebacks, and the eggs and young of larger fish such as salmon and trout.

One bold fledgling
   wanders down the creek.
It's been a long time
   since she ate from Papa's beak.
She's hungry—where is Mama,
   with dinner on the wing?
Then down between the boulders,
   she sees a wiggly thing.

It looks like a caddisfly!
   She grabs it in her bill,
Then sees another, grabs it,
   and her belly starts to fill.
Soon she learns to catch the bugs
   and fish that keep her strong.
She learns to preen her feathers
   and to sing the dipper song.

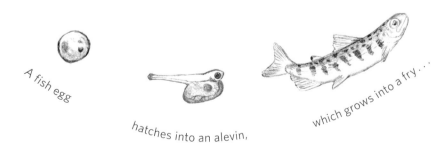

A fish egg

hatches into an alevin,

which grows into a fry . . .

. . . all of which are nutritious food for dippers.

Unlike many other small birds, dippers don't migrate long distances to warmer climates in winter. Even in the coldest months, dippers can be seen diving into the water for bugs and fish, and perched on the snowy streamside, dipping up and down.

And so when autumn rains begin,
the fledgling doesn't fret.
She knows her feathered jacket
keeps out the cold and wet.
She doesn't scurry from the rain
or hide from howling wind.
She knows the dipper's secret:
autumn rain's a dipper's friend.

Rain splashes 'cross the alder roots
   and trickles down the stones.
It tumbles into pools
   and plucks at salmon bones.
It fills the streams and rivers,
   and that's a dipper's wish:
A water-world that's right for her,
   with lots of bugs and fish.

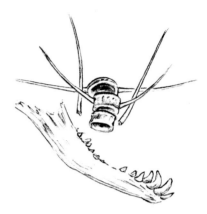

These bones are a salmon jaw and
two vertebrae.

Then, when winter closes in,
   with ice and wind and frost,
The dipper travels down the stream,
   but she isn't lost.
She makes her way along the creek,
   toward the ocean shore,
Catching fish and amphipods,
   salmon eggs, and more.

Dodging hungry goshawks
   looking for a snack,
Fleeing from a raven's
   dangerous attack,
She travels through the watersheds,
   exploring here and there,
Meeting other dippers,
   fighting for her share.

Although they don't migrate long distances for the winter, dippers do wander. They may travel through several watersheds in the nonbreeding season. In coastal areas, some even go to the ocean and find food, such as amphipods, in the seaweed.

As winter turns to spring
    and the days grow light and long,
She meets a handsome fellow;
    he sings a rollicking song.
He guards a rushing creek
    where the water's white with foam,
Where lots of bugs and sculpins
    make a proper dipper home.

They build a round and cozy nest
    deep in a boulder pile,
Weaving it with lots of moss
    (construction takes a while!).
Soon there will be eggs,
    and hungry chicks to tend,
And bugs to catch, and songs to sing,
    as the cycle starts again.

Fresh sculpin . . .

. . . a favorite dipper food.

More about American Dippers, Singers in the Stream

American dippers (*Cinclus mexicanus*) are small, gray songbirds with an unusual lifestyle: they live their whole lives near (and in!) fast-moving mountain streams. Dippers range from the mountains of northern Alaska to the mountains of southern Central America. They do not migrate to southern latitudes, though they often come down to lower elevations in winter. If you live in the dippers' range, you might have dippers in your neighborhood. You can also see dippers in many US and Canadian National Parks, including:

UNITED STATES	North Cascades
Capitol Reef	Olympic
Crater Lake	Redwood
Death Valley	Sequoia
Denali	Wrangell-St. Elias
Glacier	Yellowstone
Glacier Bay	Yosemite
Grand Canyon	Zion
Grand Teton	
Great Basin	CANADA
Katmai	Banff
Kings Canyon	Jasper
Lassen	Kluane
Mount Rainier	Waterton Lakes

Juneau, AK

Yosemite National Park, CA

▨ **Year-round**

Map courtesy of the Birds of North America;
Cornell Lab of Ornithology

Dipper Foods

Dippers feed mostly on immature (larval) aquatic insects, especially mayflies, stoneflies, and caddisflies. They also eat small fish, including sculpins, juvenile salmon, and juvenile trout. In regions where salmon spawn, dippers sometimes eat eggs that have drifted free of the gravel. And in coastal areas, they feed in the intertidal zone, eating amphipods and other tiny prey.

Since most of their prey live underwater, dippers usually find and catch their food by diving and swimming, using their wings to move through the water, and sometimes using their strong toes to grip the rocks. Sometimes they wade in the shallows, turning small stones to look underneath, or paddle along the surface with their faces in the water like snorkelers. They also pluck crawling insects from streamside vegetation, and fly up to catch insects in the air.

Songs and Calls

Dippers sing to declare their territory and to communicate with mates and potential mates. In most songbird species, only males sing. But both male and female dippers sing. The dipper song is a complex sequence of buzzy trills and bright whistles. It's often loud and clear enough to hear even over the sound of a waterfall. Although dippers sing most often during the breeding season, they will sing at other times of year as well, including the middle of winter.

Like many other bird species, dippers also have *calls*: single notes that signal alarm, or warning, or simply "I'm coming!" The dipper call is a rapid series of sharp *zeet! zeet!* sounds. The birds call at all times of the year as they fly or perch along the stream.

Glossary

alder a type of tree that often grows along streams where dippers live.

alevin very young salmon or trout that have just hatched from their eggs; they still have yolk sacs bulging out of their stomachs to nourish them until they can feed on their own.

amphipod small, aquatic, shrimp-like animals.

aquatic associated with water.

brood the group of chicks in a nest.

brood patch a bare, featherless area, well-supplied with blood vessels, that develops on the belly of a female dipper during the nesting season. It helps the female transfer her body heat to the eggs and very young chicks when she settles over them in the nest.

fry young salmon or trout a little older than alevins; the yolk sac has been absorbed; fry can feed themselves.

goshawk a medium-sized hawk that preys on small birds and squirrels in forested areas.

John Muir famous naturalist, explorer, and conservationist, who studied glaciers in Alaska and California, and ardently advocated for the preservation of Yosemite and other natural wonders.

migration regular seasonal movements of animals from one place to another.

pinfeathers very new feathers, just starting to grow, that poke out though the skin (like pins); they are enclosed in scaly sheaths.

pollutants nasty stuff that gets in the water and makes it harmful and even poisonous.

preen to clean and arrange the feathers; the preening bird dips its bill into the oil gland near the tail and spreads the oil over the feathers to help waterproof them.

riffle a shallow part of a stream where the fast water makes little waves over the rocks.

songbirds birds that have complex structures in the throat that allow them to sing elaborate songs.

water ouzel the old name for the American dipper.

watershed an area of land that all drains into a single water body, such as a river, lake, or bay.

To the dipper we called "blue white red"

Text copyright © 2008, 2015 by Katherine Hocker and Mary Willson
Illustrations copyright © 2008 by Katherine Hocker, except for the title page illustration, copyright © 2015

Published in the United States by Yosemite Conservancy.

Library of Congress Control Number: 2014942546

Cover art by Katherine Hocker
Cover design by Nancy Austin
Interior design by Katherine Hocker and Nancy Austin

ISBN 978-1-930238-56-5
First Yosemite Conservancy printing, 2015

Printed by Toppan Leefung Printing Ltd in China, October 2014

1 2 3 4 5 6 – 18 17 16 15

YOSEMITE
CONSERVANCY.

yosemiteconservancy.org

FSC
www.fsc.org

MIX
Paper from responsible sources
FSC® C104723

John Muir and Dippers

During John Muir's first summer in the Sierra, he noted a little gray bird that lived on the streams, wading and diving for its food, bobbing up and down, and singing a sweet song. He didn't have a name for it then but later learned to call it "cinclus" (its scientific name is *Cinclus mexicanus*), or by its old name "ouzel" or "water ouzel." And so it was known for decades, until its official name was changed to American dipper.

Muir learned where to look for the bird: *Find a fall, or cascade, or rushing rapid, anywhere upon a clear stream, and there you will surely find its complementary Ouzel, flitting about in the spray, diving in foaming eddies, whirling like a leaf. . . Tracing on strong wing every curve of the most precipitous torrents from one extremity of the Sierra to the other.*

It soon became Muir's favorite bird. *Among all the mountain birds,* he wrote, *none has cheered me so much in my lonely wanderings,—none so unfailingly. For both in winter and summer he sings, sweetly, cheerily. . . . The Ouzel sings on through all the seasons and every kind of storm.*

Eventually, he discovered how his favorites nested: *The Ouzel's nest is one of the most extraordinary pieces of bird architecture I ever saw, odd and novel in design, perfectly fresh and beautiful, and in every way worthy of the genius of the little builder.*

Even so far north as icy Alaska, Muir wrote, *I have found my glad singer.* With his canoe caught among the icebergs of a glacial bay, he *suddenly heard the well-known whir of an Ouzel's wings, and, looking up, saw my little comforter coming straight across the ice from the shore. In a second or two he was with me, flying three times round my head with a happy salute, as if saying, "Cheer up, old friend; you see I'm here, and all's well."*

A tough little bird, and a clever builder; bringer of song to the mountain streams, and bringer of cheer to a wilderness wanderer: *Such, then, is our little cinclus, beloved of every one who is so fortunate as to know him.*

---

against the bottom of the stream. Then we brushed the rocks and stirred up the stream bottom just upstream of the net. The water current swept any dislodged aquatic insects into the net. We emptied the net into a plastic tray, sorted the insects into different types, and counted them.

We also studied the small fish in the streams. We used collapsible minnow traps that are very light and easy to carry in a backpack. We baited the traps, tied them to rocks or branches so they didn't float away, and left them overnight. The next day, we checked them to see how many and what kinds of fish were caught, and then released the fish.

Adventures

Learning about dippers led us on many adventures. After the dippers finished nesting, we checked the nests for lining materials (soft grass) and for signs of parasites. Since dippers do such a good job of making their nests hard to reach, we had to be creative about getting to them. To get to nests that are high on cliffs, we and our helpers used climbing equipment. At least once, we had to swim to reach a nest!

In coastal Alaska, in midsummer, dipper nesting season sometimes overlaps salmon season—and that means bears are always nearby along the streams. More than once, we encountered curious bears while we sat quietly watching the dippers, and we often stepped on their big paw-prints on the trails to our study sites.

But learning about these fascinating birds was worth all the cold, and wet, and hard work. Almost every time we went out, we learned something new. We hope you are inspired to look for dippers the next time you visit a mountain stream. Who knows what you might discover. There's a lot left to learn!

Sources

Muir, John. *The Mountains of California*. New York: The Century Co., 1894.

Tyler, S. and S. Ormerod. *The Dippers*. London: T. and A.D. Poyser, 1994.

Willson, Mary and Katherine Hocker. *American Dippers—Singers in the Mountain Streams*. Juneau, AK: Cinclus Press.

Willson, Mary F. and Hugh E. Kingery. "American Dipper (*Cinclus mexicanus*)," The Birds of North America Online (A. Poole, Ed.). Ithaca: Cornell Lab of Ornithology, 2011.

Willson, Mary F. and K.M. Hocker. "Natural History of Nesting American Dippers (*Cinclus mexicanus*) in Southeastern Alaska." *Northwestern Naturalist* 89 (2008): 97–106.

Studying Dippers

We studied dippers around Juneau, Alaska, for many years. At first, our main goal was to map the distribution of dippers along streams in our area: what streams they nest on and how many pairs nest on each stream. As we did that, however, our curiosity led us to learn much more about their lives.

To study dippers, we had to get right down in the creeks with them. We spent a lot of time in chest waders, and we were often wet! In spring, we searched for dipper nests by wading in streams or hiking along streambanks, trying to follow the birds as they carried nesting material or food to their nesting sites. Sometimes it took us several days to find a nest, because the dippers can fly much faster than we can walk, and they can be hard to follow. Dippers don't put their nests near each other, but spread them out along a stream; some of the nests we studied were miles from the nearest road, so we did a lot of hiking.

Nest-Watching and Banding

After we found a nest, we visited the site every few days to check its progress. We watched nests to find out how often the parents fed the chicks, how the nest was kept clean, and if the parents successfully reared their brood until the chicks came out of the nest and hunted for their own food.

After the eggs hatched, we marked the adults so we could identify them individually. We did this by putting colorful plastic bands on their legs, with a different color combination for each bird. To catch the birds so we could band them, we stretched a net across the stream; this net is made of fine black nylon string, which is hard to see.

This dipper has three colored bands, and one aluminum band.
PHOTO: A. W. HANGER

A stonefly with a caddisfly above it.
PHOTO: KATHERINE HOCKER

When a bird flew along the stream to or from the nest, it flew right into the net (although there were always a few that were too smart for us!). We took the bird out of the net and went to shore, where we weighed it and banded it. We determined its sex by looking for bare brood patches on its belly: because only females incubate, only they have brood patches. Finally, we released the dipper. The birds got used to the bands very quickly.

Observing Banded Birds

Once the adults were banded, we could look for these individuals throughout the rest of the year. During each nesting season, we recorded which of the banded adults returned to their previous nesting territories and which ones moved to new places for nesting. We could also estimate how many dippers survived the winter from the number of banded birds that we saw again the next year.

Studying Dipper Foods

To learn about what the dippers were eating, we placed a long-handled net, specially made for this purpose,

Taking careful field notes.
PHOTO: SKIP GRAY

Removing a dipper from a net.
PHOTO: SKIP GRAY

Catching bugs.
PHOTO: CHERYL COOK

Territories and Nests

Dippers form pairs early in spring. Each pair defends a territory along a stream, vigorously chasing out any intruding dippers. Some territories are small, only a few hundred yards long, but others may be over a mile long.

Dippers nest beside streams on cliffs or under boulders, under bridges, or even behind waterfalls. Inside a ball-shaped nest of moss, a pad of grass and leaves provides a bed for the eggs and, later, the chicks. The female incubates the eggs while the male guards the nest. When the chicks hatch, they are nearly featherless and unable to keep themselves warm for the first week, so the female often sits on the chicks, with the male bringing most of the food. By the time the chicks are three weeks old, the adults may feed them as often as twenty times an hour.

Chicks

Chicks live in the nest for about three and a half weeks. During that time they grow quickly, and by the time they leave the nest, they look very much like adults, but with shorter wings and tails.

The parents continue to feed them often, but soon the youngsters start pecking at things that look like they might be food. After a few days, they are fairly proficient at identifying and catching insects. The parents may feed them for up to four weeks before they're completely on their own. If either adult is killed by a predator, the surviving parent can raise the chicks alone.

While one brood of chicks is becoming independent, the parents sometimes start a second brood, if the first brood was started early enough in the season and food is sufficiently abundant. Scientists observing dippers in Northern California found that in some years, three broods may be possible there.

Once they are independent, young dippers move away from where they were born, sometimes many miles away, seeking a place to set up their own territories and find a mate. They can nest and raise chicks when they are one year old. Like most small birds, dippers have short lives compared to humans. Most dippers don't live more than three or four years.

Late Summer, Fall, and Winter

After the nesting season, dippers often travel to other streams, mountain lakes, or estuaries to hunt for food.

Staying Warm

Dippers live along—and in—streams that are cold throughout the year. Because they're quite small (an adult dipper is smaller than a robin; it would fit in a hand like a baseball), cold is even more of a danger to them than it is to larger animals. To survive in their cold habitat, dippers must stay warm and dry, and eat plenty of food. Their plumage helps: they have unusually dense feathers, which require lots of preening and anointing with oil from large glands near their tails. They forage all day long; it takes a lot of food to sustain them through the winter. Long spells of very cold weather, when the streams freeze, can make it especially hard for the dippers to get enough food.

Healthy Streams, Healthy Dippers

Dippers are good indicators of healthy streams. Polluted waters support fewer insects, so there is less food available and fewer chicks survive. Furthermore, the adults accumulate certain pollutants in their bodies, which affects their own health. When streams become too polluted, dippers cannot live there.

Dippers are experts at catching aquatic insects.
PHOTO: A. W. HANGER

An adult bringing food to a nest, where chicks gape their yellow beaks.
PHOTO: KATHERINE HOCKER

A dipper in winter, keeping one leg warm by tucking it in its soft feathers.
PHOTO: BOB ARMSTRONG